THE CELEBRITY BRANDING BLUEPRINT

DR. CATRISE AUSTIN

Dentist to the Stars

TABLE OF CONTENTS:

TABLE OF CONTENTS: i

The Celebrity Branding Blueprint – How to Build Influence, Monetize Your Brand, and Create a Legacy? vi

Why You Need to Think Like a Celebrity When Building Your Brand vi

What This Book Will Teach You vii

Who This Book is For viii

How to Get the Most Out of This Book ix

Are You Ready to Build a Brand That Lasts? x

The Power of Personal Branding – How Celebrities Build Influence and Authority 1

Why Personal Branding is the Key to Success 1

What Makes Celebrities So Influential? 3

The Three Pillars of a Powerful Personal Brand 4

Action Steps: Build Your Celebrity-Level Personal Brand 6

What's Next? 7

Crafting Your Signature Image – How to Become Instantly Recognizable 9

Why Your Image Matters in Personal Branding 9

The Biggest Mistakes Entrepreneurs Make with Their Image 10

How to Develop Your Signature Brand Image 11

The Psychology Behind Image and Branding 13

Action Steps: Build Your Signature Brand Image 14

What's Next? 15

The Art of Storytelling – How to Connect with Your Audience 17

Why Storytelling is the Most Powerful Branding Tool 17

How to Craft a Brand Story That Resonates 18

3 Key Elements of a Powerful Brand Story 19

Using Storytelling Across Your Brand 20

Social Media – Make Your Story Part of Your Content Strategy 21

Public Speaking – Captivate Your Audience with Stories 21

Marketing – Emotion Sells More Than Logic 22

Action Steps – Craft Your Signature Brand Story 22

What's Next? 23

What's Next? 27

Social Media Domination – How to Grow Your Audience with Celebrity-Level Strategies 28

Why Social Media is the Ultimate Brand-Building Tool 28

The Most Common Social Media Mistakes That Kill Growth 30

The Celebrity Social Media Playbook – 5 Proven Strategies....................31

Action Steps – Build Your Celebrity-Level Social Media Strategy..............34

What's Next?...35

The Power of Celebrity Endorsements – How to Use Star-Level Marketing for Your Brand 37

Why Celebrity Endorsements Drive Massive Brand Growth.....................37

Why Celebrity Partnerships Work (And Why Consumers Trust Them)...39

What This Means for Entrepreneurs & Small Business Owners................40

How to Secure High-Value Brand Partnerships (Even Without Millions of Followers)..40

Monetizing Brand Endorsements – Turning Partnerships into Revenue 43

Action Steps – Secure Your First (or Next) Brand Deal..............................44

What's Next?...45

The Celebrity Marketing Playbook – How A-List Stars Build Massive Brand Loyalty 47

Why Brand Loyalty is the Ultimate Competitive Advantage......................47

The Biggest Brand Loyalty Mistakes That Kill Customer Retention..........48

The Most Common Mistakes That Hurt Brand Loyalty..............................49

The Celebrity Brand Loyalty Formula – 5 Key Strategies..........................50

Action Steps – Build a Loyal Fan Base for Your Brand...............................55

What's Next? 56

How Celebrities Build Massive Fan Bases (And How You Can Too) 58

The Secret to Turning Followers Into Devoted Fans 58

The Biggest Mistakes That Prevent You From Growing a Loyal Audience 61

The Celebrity Blueprint for Building a Devoted Fan Base 62

Action Steps – Grow a Devoted Fan Base Like a Celebrity 67

What's Next? 68

Authenticity vs. Curation – How Celebrities Balance Realness and Perfection in Branding 70

The Fine Line Between Being Real and Being Polished 70

The Biggest Authenticity Mistakes That Hurt Your Brand 74

How Celebrities Balance Authenticity and Curation 75

Action Steps – Master the Art of Authenticity & Curation 81

What's Next? 81

The Power of Personal Reinvention – How Celebrities Stay Relevant for Decades 83

Why Reinvention is the Key to Longevity in Your Brand 83

The Biggest Reinvention Mistakes That Kill a Brand 86

The Celebrity Formula for Staying Relevant 87

Action Steps – Successfully Reinvent Your Brand Without Losing Your Audience 97

What's Next? 97

The Celebrity Business Empire – How to Turn Your Personal Brand Into Multiple Streams of Income 99

Why Every Strong Personal Brand Needs Multiple Income Streams 99

The Biggest Mistakes That Keep Entrepreneurs Stuck in One Income Stream 103

How Celebrities Monetize Their Personal Brands 104

Action Steps – Turn Your Personal Brand Into an Empire 120

What's Next? 121

Wrapping It All Together & Taking Action Like a Celebrity Brand Builder 122

The Roadmap to Building a Powerful, Profitable Personal Brand 122

Taking the Next Step – Where Do You Go From Here? 126

Let's Work Together – Build Your Brand Like a Celebrity 127

About The Author 130

INTRODUCTION

The Celebrity Branding Blueprint – How to Build Influence, Monetize Your Brand, and Create a Legacy?

Why You Need to Think Like a Celebrity When Building Your Brand

What separates celebrities from everyday entrepreneurs, coaches, and business owners? **It's not just talent—it's branding.**

Think about the biggest names in entertainment, business, and media—**Oprah, Rihanna, Kevin Hart, Dr. Dre, Taylor Swift.** These icons didn't just rely on their craft; they **built powerful personal brands that commanded attention, trust, and loyalty.**

Now, here's the truth most people don't realize:

You don't have to be famous to build a brand like a celebrity.

In today's digital world, **personal branding is the key to influence, income, and long-term success.** Whether you're an entrepreneur, influencer, coach, or creative, you need a brand that:

→ Makes you instantly recognizable in your industry.

→ Attracts opportunities, clients, and partnerships effortlessly.

→ Positions you as an authority, so people listen when you speak.

→ Generates multiple streams of income beyond just your main business.

"Success isn't just about what you do—it's about how the world perceives you."

If you want to build a **powerful, profitable personal brand**, it's time to start thinking like the most successful celebrities in the world. This book will show you exactly how to do it.

What This Book Will Teach You

This isn't just another branding book full of generic advice. This is a **celebrity-inspired strategy guide** that will help you:

→ Craft a brand identity that makes you stand out.

- → Master social media, storytelling, and audience engagement.

- → Build a loyal fan base that actively supports your brand.

- → Monetize your brand through multiple income streams.

- → Stay relevant and reinvent yourself as your industry evolves.

Each chapter is designed to give you the exact strategies celebrities use to stay at the top of their game—and show you how to apply them to your own brand, business, and career.

Who This Book is For

This book is for anyone who wants to build a **recognizable, influential, and highly profitable personal brand.**

- **Entrepreneurs** looking to attract more clients, partnerships, and revenue.

- **Coaches, speakers, and consultants** who want to position themselves as industry leaders.

- **Influencers and creatives** who want to grow their audience and monetize their brand.

- **Experts and professionals** who want to increase their visibility and authority.

If you're ready to start building a brand that **commands attention, creates impact, and generates income**, this book will give you the blueprint to make it happen.

How to Get the Most Out of This Book

Each chapter will walk you through **celebrity-inspired branding strategies**—but this isn't just a book to read. It's a **book to take action on.**

Here's how to get the best results:

1. **Read each chapter with a business mindset.** Think about how you can apply these strategies to your brand.

2. **Take notes and create an action plan.** Don't just consume information—start implementing it.

3. **Follow the step-by-step exercises.** At the end of each chapter, you'll find actionable steps to help you apply what you've learned.

4. **Commit to executing.** The difference between successful personal brands and those who get stuck? **Action.**

Are You Ready to Build a Brand That Lasts?

The most powerful personal brands aren't built overnight—but with the right strategy, **you can create a brand that opens doors, generates wealth, and cements your legacy.**

This book will show you how to **do it the celebrity way.**

Turn the page, and let's get started.

CHAPTER 1

The Power of Personal Branding – How Celebrities Build Influence and Authority

Why Personal Branding is the Key to Success

Personal branding is no longer just for celebrities and Fortune 500 CEOs. In today's digital world, it's what separates those who stand out from those who get overlooked. Whether you're an entrepreneur, speaker, content creator, or business owner, **your personal brand is your most valuable asset.**

Think about the most recognizable figures in entertainment, business, and media. **Oprah Winfrey, Beyoncé, and Dwayne "The Rock" Johnson** are not just famous; they have built **powerful personal brands that make them unforgettable.**

A personal brand isn't just about how you look or what you do—it's about **the perception you create and the impact you make.** It's the reputation that follows you wherever you go. If you don't define your brand, the world will define it for you.

When you take control of your personal brand, you can:

- Position yourself as a **leader in your industry**

- Attract **more opportunities and high-value clients**

- Build **trust, authority, and credibility**

- Create a **legacy that extends beyond your career**

A strong personal brand isn't about fame—it's about influence, positioning, and long-term success.

"Your personal brand is what people say about you when you're not in the room." – Jeff Bezos

What Makes Celebrities So Influential?

Most entrepreneurs and professionals struggle with **visibility and credibility**. They have expertise, but they lack a clear message and strategy to stand out. Celebrities don't have that problem—because they have mastered **brand positioning, storytelling, and consistency.**

- **Oprah Winfrey** built an empire on **authenticity, empowerment, and trust.** She didn't just host a talk show—she became the brand.

- **Beyoncé** represents excellence, **work ethic, and creativity.** Her name alone evokes an emotional connection with her audience.

- **Dwayne Johnson** turned his wrestling persona into a **global brand that extends into fitness, Hollywood, and entrepreneurship.**

These individuals didn't wait for the world to recognize them. They **created a brand identity that made them impossible to ignore.** Their success wasn't just about talent—it was about intentional brand-building.

The good news? **You can apply the same principles to your own brand, no matter your industry.**

The Three Pillars of a Powerful Personal Brand

Building a personal brand requires **clarity, consistency, and visibility.** The most successful brands—whether they belong to celebrities, business leaders, or entrepreneurs—are built on three key pillars:

1. Identity – Define Who You Are and What You Stand For

Your personal brand starts with **clarity.** Who are you? What do you stand for? What message do you want people to associate with you?

Successful personal brands have a strong identity that is:

- Authentic and aligned with their values
- Clear and easy to recognize
- Consistently reinforced through messaging and visuals

Before you can market yourself effectively, you must define **who you are, what you offer, and why people should trust you.**

2. Storytelling – Create an Emotional Connection

People don't connect with businesses; they connect with stories. The most influential personal brands use storytelling to create an emotional bond with their audience.

Your brand story should:

- Showcase your **journey**, challenges, and transformation
- Explain **why you do what you do**
- Position you as **relatable, trustworthy, and aspirational**

Oprah's brand story is built on overcoming adversity. Beyoncé's brand story is about discipline and reinvention. The best personal brands **use their story to inspire, connect, and attract their audience.**

3. Consistency – Show Up and Stay Relevant

A weak brand is inconsistent. A strong brand is **reliable, recognizable, and always present.**

- Beyoncé doesn't randomly change her image or messaging every few months.
- Oprah has been **reinforcing empowerment and personal growth for decades.**
- Dwayne Johnson **consistently delivers motivation, fitness inspiration, and leadership lessons.**

The key to branding success? **Repetition and reliability.** If you're constantly changing your message, style, or brand identity, people will struggle to trust and remember you.

Action Steps: Build Your Celebrity-Level Personal Brand

If you want to build a personal brand that attracts attention, creates impact, and grows your influence, take these steps:

- → **Define Your Brand Identity** – Clarify your values, mission, and what makes you unique.

- → **Craft Your Brand Story** – Write out your journey in a way that connects with your audience.

- → **Identify Your Target Audience** – Who are your "fans," and how can you serve them?

- → **Commit to Consistency** – Show up regularly and ensure your messaging is clear and cohesive.

Your personal brand is the foundation for **building trust, attracting clients, and becoming an authority in your industry.** The more intentional you are about shaping it, the faster you'll see results.

What's Next?

Now that you understand the power of personal branding and how celebrities use it to build massive influence, it's time to take it a step further. A strong brand isn't just about what you say—it's also about how you show up, present yourself, and make a lasting impression.

Think about the most recognizable celebrities and industry leaders. You can spot them before they even say a word. Their signature style, presence, and overall image tell a story that aligns perfectly with their brand.

→ **Janelle Monáe** – Her signature black-and-white aesthetic isn't just a fashion choice—it's a visual representation of her brand's themes of identity, rebellion, and artistic expression. She has crafted an image that is instantly recognizable while remaining deeply authentic.

→ **Erykah Badu** – Whether it's her towering headwraps or her ethereal, bohemian style, Badu's look is as much a part of her brand as her music, reinforcing her identity as a cultural and spiritual icon.

→ **Anna Wintour** – Her sleek bob and signature sunglasses aren't just a fashion statement—they are a symbol of power, exclusivity, and influence in the fashion industry.

This isn't by accident—it's intentional brand identity. The way you present yourself online, in media appearances, or even at networking events should reinforce the message of your brand and make you stand out in a crowded space.

In the next chapter, we'll dive into Crafting Your Signature Image – How to Become Instantly Recognizable.

You'll learn:

- How to define a signature style that aligns with your brand.

- How visual branding and consistency help you stand out.

- Why first impressions matter—and how to make yours unforgettable.

Because in today's world, **people see you before they hear you.** It's time to make sure your brand image is working for you, not against you.

Get ready—because your transformation into an **iconic brand presence** starts now.

CHAPTER 2

Crafting Your Signature Image – How to Become Instantly Recognizable

Why Your Image Matters in Personal Branding

Your personal brand is not just about what you say—it's about how people perceive you before you even speak. First impressions are formed within seconds, and in the digital age, your **visual identity is one of the most powerful tools** for influencing how people view your brand.

The most iconic personal brands—**Beyoncé, Tom Ford, and Cardi B**—are instantly recognizable. Their signature styles reinforce their brand identity, making them memorable across industries. Beyoncé exudes **polished excellence and luxury**, Tom Ford embodies **sleek minimalism and timeless fashion**, while **Cardi B's bold, unapologetic image** reflects her brand of authenticity and high energy.

These aren't just personal style choices. **They are branding strategies.** A carefully crafted image creates consistency, trust, and a lasting impression. If you want to stand out, you must be intentional about the way you present yourself to the world.

The Biggest Mistakes Entrepreneurs Make with Their Image

While celebrities spend years refining their brand image, many entrepreneurs and professionals **fail to create a cohesive and recognizable visual identity.** Here's where they go wrong:

- **Inconsistency** – Changing up branding elements too often confuses your audience and weakens brand recognition.

- **Copying Instead of Creating** – Trying to imitate someone else's look instead of developing an authentic image leads to forgettable branding.

- **Neglecting Visuals** – Low-quality images, outdated headshots, or mismatched branding weaken credibility and make it harder for people to take you seriously.

Celebrities don't leave their brand image to chance. **They make every detail—from their wardrobe to their color palette—part of a larger brand story.** You should do the same.

How to Develop Your Signature Brand Image

Your **visual presence should align with your brand message.** Whether you want to be seen as innovative, luxurious, approachable, or authoritative, your image should reinforce that perception. Here's how:

Step 1 – Define Your Visual Identity

A strong brand image begins with clarity. Before making decisions about your wardrobe, branding colors, or social media aesthetics, **define the message you want to send.** Ask yourself:

- What colors and styles best represent my brand?
- What emotions do I want my brand to evoke?
- How do I want people to describe my presence and appearance?

Your brand identity should be **intentional**, not accidental. **If you are a luxury brand, your aesthetic should reflect elegance.** If your brand is built on **innovation**, your image should be **modern and cutting-edge.**

Step 2 – Maintain a Cohesive Aesthetic Across All Platforms

Your audience should recognize your brand instantly, whether they see you on Instagram, LinkedIn, a website, or a conference stage. **Consistency builds trust.**

- **Color Palette:** Use 2-3 core brand colors across all platforms.
- **Photography Style:** High-quality, professional headshots and lifestyle photos reinforce your credibility.
- **Social Media Branding:** Maintain a consistent aesthetic in visuals, fonts, and tone.

When your branding is cohesive, people start associating specific visuals with your name—a powerful asset in standing out.

Step 3 – Create a Signature Look & Style

A signature look isn't just about fashion—it's about creating a **recognizable visual identity**. Steve Jobs was known for his black turtleneck. Anna Wintour is rarely seen without her bob haircut and dark sunglasses. These **details become part of their brand DNA.**

- Is there a specific **outfit, accessory, or hairstyle that makes you stand out?**

- Do you have a **signature color or pattern** that people associate with you?

- How does your on-**camera or stage presence** reinforce your brand's energy?

Your personal style should complement your brand's messaging. If you are positioning yourself as an expert, your attire should reflect authority and confidence. If your brand is about innovation and creativity, your visuals should be fresh and dynamic.

> <u>Pro Tip:</u>
>
> If you're unsure about your brand's aesthetic, study leaders in your industry. Identify what makes them visually recognizable and apply those insights to create a look that is uniquely yours.

The Psychology Behind Image and Branding

Studies show that it takes only **seven seconds to make a first impression.** People subconsciously judge credibility, authority, and trustworthiness based on **visual cues.**

When you craft a strong brand image:

- You **appear more authoritative and credible.**

- You **attract an audience that aligns with your message.**

- You **reinforce trust and make yourself more memorable.**

This is why luxury brands maintain a **refined aesthetic**, while tech brands lean toward **sleek, minimalist designs**. Your image should reflect the perception you want to create.

"Your brand is what people say about you when you're not in the room, and your image is what they notice first."

Action Steps: Build Your Signature Brand Image

To take control of your personal brand's visual identity, implement these key steps:

1. **Define Your Color Palette and Aesthetic** – Choose 2-3 core brand colors that align with your message.

2. **Develop a Personal Style Guide** – Outline your wardrobe, accessories, and overall style for brand consistency.

3. **Invest in Professional Branding Photography** – High-quality images elevate your authority and brand perception.

4. **Audit Your Online Presence** – Ensure that your website, social media, and marketing visuals are aligned.

5. **Commit to a Consistent Image** – Whether online or in person, your brand aesthetic should always match your message.

What's Next?

By now, you've laid the foundation of your personal brand and crafted a signature image that makes you instantly recognizable. But here's the thing—a strong brand isn't just about how you look; it's about the story you tell.

Every iconic celebrity and industry leader—from Oprah to Tyler Perry, Beyoncé to Steve Jobs—has mastered the art of storytelling to build a deep emotional connection with their audience. Why? Because people don't just buy products or services—they buy into stories.

Your audience wants to know:

→ Who are you beyond your brand image?

→ What challenges have shaped your journey?

→ Why should they trust and connect with you?

A great story makes you **relatable, memorable, and impactful**. It turns casual followers into loyal fans, clients into brand ambassadors, and opportunities into long-term success.

In Chapter 3, we'll uncover The Art of Storytelling – How to Connect with Your Audience. You'll learn how to craft and share a personal brand story that not only **captures attention but builds trust, influence, and lasting loyalty.**

Because when you master storytelling, **you don't just build a brand— you create a movement.**

CHAPTER 3

The Art of Storytelling – How to Connect with Your Audience

Why Storytelling is the Most Powerful Branding Tool

Behind every great brand is a **great story**. The most influential figures—whether in entertainment, business, or media—aren't just known for what they do; they're remembered for the **stories they tell.**

Think about **Oprah Winfrey.** Her story of overcoming poverty and trauma to become one of the most influential media moguls in history is what makes her brand so powerful. It's not just about her success—it's about the emotional connection she builds with her audience. **Steve Jobs** didn't just create Apple; he created a movement around the idea of innovation, simplicity, and challenging the status quo. **Tyler Perry** turned his personal struggles into films and plays that deeply resonate with his audience.

These individuals didn't just build businesses or careers; they built emotional connections. Storytelling isn't just about sharing information—it's about **making people feel something**. It turns a personal brand into something **memorable, impactful, and influential**.

"People don't buy products or services—they buy the stories behind them."

Yet, many entrepreneurs struggle with storytelling because they don't know how to craft a compelling narrative. Instead of drawing people in, their messaging feels **generic, overly polished, or disconnected from their audience**. The truth is storytelling isn't about having the most dramatic past or the perfect way with words—it's about **sharing your journey in a way that is authentic, relatable, and valuable to others**.

How to Craft a Brand Story That Resonates

A great brand story isn't just about where you started—it's about the **journey, the challenges, and the transformation** that shaped who you are today. The most impactful personal brands are built on **narratives that show struggle, growth, and triumph**.

One of the biggest mistakes in branding is making the story too focused on **yourself** rather than your audience. The most effective brand stories invite people in, making them feel like they are a part of the journey. **Tyler Perry doesn't just tell his personal story—he shares experiences that reflect the lives of his audience, creating a deep emotional connection.** Michelle Obama does the same, using her personal struggles and triumphs to inspire people from all walks of life.

3 Key Elements of a Powerful Brand Story

1. Authenticity – Be Real, Not Perfect

Your audience doesn't expect perfection—they expect **authenticity**. The most powerful brand stories don't hide struggles; they highlight them.

Consider **Sara Blakely, the founder of Spanx**. She openly shares how she started with just $5,000, faced rejection from male-dominated boardrooms, and built a billion-dollar empire. Her transparency made her brand **relatable and trustworthy**.

2. Relatability – Make It About Your Audience, Not Just You

Your story isn't just about you—it's about how **your journey relates to your audience**.

The reason **Tyler Perry's films** have such a loyal fan base is that they speak directly to the experiences of his audience. He understands their struggles, aspirations, and emotions.

3. Transformation – Show the Before and After

Every powerful story has a **before and after moment.**

Oprah Winfrey's story isn't just about where she is today—it's about how she overcame poverty and trauma to become one of the most influential figures in media. That transformation is what makes her story **inspiring and powerful.**

> Pro Tip:
>
> When crafting your brand story, start with a defining moment—a challenge, a realization, or a breakthrough that changed your path. This is what makes a story compelling.

Using Storytelling Across Your Brand

Once you have crafted your brand story, the next step is integrating it into everything you do. A powerful story shouldn't just live on the "About Me" page of your website—it should be woven into your **content, marketing, speeches, and even casual conversations.**

Social Media – Make Your Story Part of Your Content Strategy

One of the most effective ways to use storytelling is through **social media**. People engage more with content that feels **personal and authentic, rather than overly promotional**. Instead of just talking about what you do, **share the story behind why you do it**.

Ways to incorporate storytelling on social media:

- Share the **behind-the-scenes** struggles and victories that brought you to where you are today.

- Post about pivotal career moments, lessons learned, and personal growth experiences.

- Create **engaging captions that tell a story** instead of just selling a product or service.

Public Speaking – Captivate Your Audience with Stories

Storytelling is a game-changer in **public speaking**. The best speakers don't just list facts or strategies—they use **personal stories to create emotional impact**.

- **Michelle Obama's speeches** are filled with personal experiences that inspire and connect.

- **Tyler Perry uses storytelling** to bring his personal struggles and triumphs to life, making his audience feel seen and understood.

If you want to be **memorable** in media interviews, keynotes, or podcasts, **lead with a compelling story.**

Marketing – Emotion Sells More Than Logic

Your brand should make people **feel something.**

- Share **behind-the-scenes moments** that humanize your brand.
- Talk about the **lessons you've learned from failure.**
- Create content that speaks directly to **your audience's aspirations and fears.**

The more **emotionally invested** people are in your story, the more they will trust and support your brand.

Action Steps – Craft Your Signature Brand Story

If you haven't defined your personal brand story yet, start by mapping out the **key moments in your journey.** Think about the pivotal experiences that shaped your values, the obstacles that challenged you, and the transformation that brought you to where you are today.

Ask Yourself These Questions:

- What inspired you to do what you do?
- What challenges did you have to overcome?
- What lessons have you learned that can help others?
- How does your story connect with your audience?

Once you have your story, **practice telling it in different formats**. Write it in a way that fits your website bio, share pieces of it on social media, and use it in networking situations. **The more you share it, the more naturally it will become part of your brand.**

"Facts tell, but stories sell. If you want people to remember you, make them feel something."

What's Next?

Now that you've defined your brand identity, crafted a signature image, and mastered the art of storytelling, it's time to take the next critical step—**getting your message in front of the right audience.**

Having a powerful brand story is one thing, but if no one hears it, **does it really make an impact?**

This is where **social media domination comes in.**

Celebrities, influencers, and industry leaders **don't just rely on traditional media to grow their audience**—they leverage social media to connect with millions, build authority, and create movements. Think about:

→ **Cardi B**, who turned her raw, unfiltered personality into a social media empire long before she became a Grammy-winning artist.

→ **Tabitha Brown**, who skyrocketed from an aspiring actress to a viral sensation and business mogul by simply sharing her authenticity on TikTok.

→ **Gary Vee**, who built his business by delivering value-packed, no-nonsense content across every major platform.

They don't just post content—they strategically position themselves, engage their audience, and turn followers into loyal brand advocates.

What's Next?

Now that you've crafted a powerful brand story and a signature image, it's time to **get seen.**

Social media isn't just a tool—it's a **launchpad** for influence, authority, and business growth. But the key isn't just posting—it's **positioning.** The most successful personal brands—**Dwayne "The Rock" Johnson, Issa Rae, and Tabitha Brown**—use social media strategically to attract opportunities, build trust, and turn followers into loyal fans.

In Chapter 4, we'll dive into Social Media Domination – How to Grow Your Audience with Celebrity-Level Strategies.

You'll learn how to:

- **Choose the right platforms** for your brand and industry
- **Create content that builds influence and engagement**
- **Leverage algorithms, trends, and consistency** to maximize your reach

Your audience is already looking for what you offer. Now, it's time to show up, stand out, and own your digital presence like a true celebrity brand.

CHAPTER 4

Social Media Domination – How to Grow Your Audience with Celebrity-Level Strategies

Why Social Media is the Ultimate Brand-Building Tool

In today's digital age, **social media is your stage**. It's where brands are built, audiences are engaged, and influence is cultivated. The right strategy can turn an unknown entrepreneur into an industry authority, just as it has for some of the most recognized names in the world.

Celebrities like **Kim Kardashian, Will Smith, and Gary Vee** have mastered social media by understanding how to create engaging content, interact with their fans, and leverage their platforms for business opportunities. **They don't just post; they strategize.**

But here's where most entrepreneurs struggle: they use social media **without a clear brand strategy.** They post inconsistently, lack a strong brand voice, and fail to create the type of content that builds loyalty and engagement.

If you want to **grow your brand like a celebrity**, you need a social media strategy that is **consistent, engaging, and aligned with your brand identity.**

"Your brand is the single most important investment you can make in your business." – Steve Forbes

---

The Most Common Social Media Mistakes That Kill Growth

Many people approach social media without a clear plan, leading to wasted effort and frustration. Here are the biggest mistakes that **prevent brand growth:**

- **Inconsistent Posting:** Without a steady presence, your audience forgets about you.

- **Lack of Engagement:** Posting isn't enough—you need to interact with your audience.

- **No Clear Brand Identity:** Random content confuses your audience and weakens your credibility.

- **Focusing Only on Sales:** Social media is about relationship-building, not just selling.

- **Ignoring Video Content:** Platforms like TikTok, Instagram Reels, and YouTube reward video over static posts.

If you're making these mistakes, don't worry—celebrities and top influencers follow **specific strategies** to dominate their space, and you can too.

The Celebrity Social Media Playbook – 5 Proven Strategies

1. Master Your Content Pillars

Celebrities and influencers don't just post whatever comes to mind— they stick to **content themes** that align with their brand. These are called **content pillars.**

For example:

- **Kim Kardashian's brand** revolves around beauty, fashion, and lifestyle.
- **Will Smith focuses on motivation, humor, and behind-the-scenes** insights.
- **Gary Vee's** content pillars include **entrepreneurship, motivation, and marketing.**

To build a strong brand, identify **3-5 core topics** that you will consistently post about.

2. Show Up Consistently & Stay Visible

If you disappear for weeks at a time, your audience will move on. **Celebrities remain in the public eye by consistently creating content.** Even if they're not promoting a project, they stay visible through behind-the-scenes posts, personal insights, and engagement with fans.

- **Post daily or at least 3-5 times per week** to stay top-of-mind.
- **Use Stories, Reels, and Live videos** to boost engagement.
- **Repurpose content across platforms** (e.g., turn a YouTube video into Instagram clips and tweets).

3. Engage With Your Audience Like a Star

The biggest celebrities make their fans feel **seen and valued**. Social media is not just a broadcast platform—it's a **two-way conversation**.

- **Respond to comments and DMs** to build relationships.
- **Ask questions** in your captions to encourage engagement.
- **Use Instagram polls and Q&As** to interact with your followers.

When your audience feels connected to you, they will **support your brand, share your content, and become your advocates.**

4. Leverage Video – The Most Powerful Engagement Tool

Video content dominates social media. TikTok, Instagram Reels, YouTube Shorts, and Facebook Live **all prioritize video over other content types.**

Why? **Video builds trust faster.** Seeing your face and hearing your voice makes your audience feel like they know you.

- **Record short-form videos (15-60 seconds) showcasing quick tips or insights.**
- **Go live regularly** to connect with your audience in real time.
- **Use storytelling in your videos** to make them engaging and shareable.

5. Monetize Your Social Media Like a Celebrity

Celebrities don't just post for fun—they turn their online presence into revenue. Whether through sponsorships, digital products, or exclusive memberships, they leverage their audience for financial success.

- **Brand Collaborations:** Partner with companies that align with your brand.
- **Digital Products:** Sell e-books, courses, or memberships.

- **Exclusive Access:** Offer behind-the-scenes content for a premium price.

Even if you're just starting out, you can **position yourself as an authority** and attract business opportunities through a well-executed social media strategy.

Action Steps – Build Your Celebrity-Level Social Media Strategy

It's time to take action. Follow these steps to optimize your social media presence:

1. **Define Your Content Pillars** – Choose 3-5 core topics that align with your brand.

2. **Post Consistently** – Aim for daily posts or at least 3-5 times per week.

3. **Engage With Your Audience** – Respond to comments, go live, and ask interactive questions.

4. **Prioritize Video Content** – Record Reels, TikToks, or YouTube Shorts to boost visibility.

5. **Leverage Your Platform for Monetization** – Explore brand deals, digital products, or exclusive memberships.

What's Next?

You've built a strong personal brand, crafted your signature image, mastered storytelling, and expanded your audience through social media. Now, it's time to take things to the next level by leveraging the power of association.

Celebrity endorsements aren't just for Hollywood stars. The most successful brands—both big and small—use strategic partnerships to elevate their credibility, expand their reach, and increase revenue.

Think about:

→ **Michael Jordan & Nike** – A partnership that turned Air Jordans into a global phenomenon.

→ **Serena Williams & Gatorade** – An alignment of power, performance, and influence.

→ **Beyoncé & Pepsi** – A multi-year endorsement deal that aligned Pepsi with Beyoncé's global influence, using her star power to drive brand visibility and engagement.

These deals weren't just about a paycheck—they were about **mutual benefit and strategic brand alignment**. The same strategies celebrities use to secure multi-million-dollar brand partnerships can be **applied to entrepreneurs, coaches, and business owners.**

In Chapter 5, we'll dive into The Power of Celebrity Endorsements – How to Use Star-Level Marketing for Your Brand.

You'll learn:

- How celebrities land major brand deals—and what makes them valuable to companies.

- How to position yourself for high-value partnerships in your industry.

- How to leverage endorsements (even without a celebrity budget) to build trust, credibility, and sales.

You don't need millions of followers or an A-list name to secure brand deals—you just need the right strategy. Let's unlock the power of endorsements and position your brand for next-level success.

CHAPTER 5

The Power of Celebrity Endorsements – How to Use Star-Level Marketing for Your Brand

Why Celebrity Endorsements Drive Massive Brand Growth

From sneakers to skincare, celebrity endorsements have the power to turn products into **multi-million-dollar brands overnight**. The reason? **People trust familiar faces.**

Jennifer Lopez & Versace – When Jennifer Lopez wore the **iconic green Versace dress** at the Grammys, it didn't just make headlines—it made history. That moment **led to a long-term collaboration with the luxury brand**, reinforcing her influence in fashion and cementing Versace's status in pop culture.

Similarly, **Michael Jordan's Air Jordan partnership with Nike** is one of the most successful celebrity-brand collaborations in history, turning his name into a global brand synonymous with excellence and style.

The good news? **You don't have to be a celebrity to leverage this strategy.** Whether you're an entrepreneur, business owner, or influencer, **you can apply the same principles of celebrity endorsements to build brand credibility, attract high-value partnerships, and skyrocket your business growth.**

"If people like you, they will listen to you. If they trust you, they will do business with you." – Zig Ziglar

---

Why Celebrity Partnerships Work (And Why Consumers Trust Them)

Celebrity endorsements work because they tap into a **psychological principle** called **social proof**. People are more likely to trust and buy a product if they see **someone they admire using it**.

For example:

- **Beyoncé's collaboration with Adidas (Ivy Park)** boosted sales by positioning the brand as **trendy and fashion-forward**.

- **George Clooney's partnership with Nespresso** added sophistication and credibility to the coffee brand.

- **Dwayne "The Rock" Johnson's Under Armour** collection strengthened the brand's image as a **go-to for high-performance athletes**.

These partnerships work because celebrities **lend their credibility, trust, and influence to brands, making them instantly more desirable**.

What This Means for Entrepreneurs & Small Business Owners

Even if you're not working with a global superstar, you can still **leverage the power of endorsements in your brand strategy.**

Here's how:

- Partner with **micro-influencers** who have engaged niche audiences.

- Get testimonials from **industry leaders, media personalities, or recognizable figures in your space.**

- Position yourself as an **authority so that brands and influencers want to collaborate with YOU.**

How to Secure High-Value Brand Partnerships (Even Without Millions of Followers)

1. Build a Personal Brand That Attracts Collaboration

Before brands or influencers will work with you, they need to see you as credible, professional, and influential in your niche.

To do this:

- **Develop a strong online presence** showcasing your expertise.

- **Create valuable content** that positions you as an industry leader.
- **Engage with brands online** before pitching—like, comment, and interact with their content.

If brands see your name consistently and recognize your expertise, they'll be more likely to consider working with you.

2. Find the Right Brand Fit

Not every brand collaboration is a good one. The best endorsements feel **authentic, aligned, and natural.**

Ask yourself:

- **Would I personally use or recommend this product?**
- **Does this brand align with my audience and values?**
- **Does this partnership feel natural, or would it seem forced?**

When endorsements feel **genuine, they create real influence.** Forced or irrelevant partnerships, on the other hand, **damage credibility and erode trust.**

3. Pitch Yourself as a Valuable Partner

Once you've identified potential brands to collaborate with, the next step is **making them see why you're the right person to represent them.**

Here's how to craft an irresistible pitch:

- Start with **why your brand aligns with theirs** (Example: "I've been a fan of your brand for years, and my audience aligns perfectly with your target customer.")

- Highlight your **audience reach and engagement**. Even with a small following, high engagement is valuable.

- Offer **value beyond exposure**. Can you create content, host an event, or bring in new customers?

> **Pro Tip:**
>
> If you don't have a large following, focus on your **credibility, expertise, and unique audience**. Many brands prefer **micro-influencers** because they often have **more engaged, loyal communities** than big-name influencers.

Monetizing Brand Endorsements – Turning Partnerships into Revenue

Once you've secured brand collaborations, it's time to **maximize their value.**

1. Leverage Your Partnerships for More Opportunities

One brand deal can **lead to more deals** if you play your cards right. Once you've completed a collaboration:

- **Share the results** (increased sales, brand exposure, etc.) to attract future partners.
- **Ask for referrals** from the brand's marketing team.
- **Use case studies and testimonials** to strengthen future pitches.

2. Turn Brand Collaborations into Recurring Income

Instead of one-off collaborations, **position yourself for long-term partnerships.**

How?

- Offer **retainer deals** (e.g., a monthly sponsorship instead of a one-time post).

- Negotiate **performance-based bonuses** (e.g., commission on sales).

- Develop **co-branded products or digital offerings** with the brand.

The more strategic you are, the more **brand partnerships can become a consistent revenue stream.**

Action Steps – Secure Your First (or Next) Brand Deal

Ready to land high-value partnerships? Follow these steps:

1. **Build Your Brand Authority** – Develop your online presence and become recognizable in your niche.

2. **Identify Aligned Brands** – Make a list of brands that match your values and audience.

3. **Engage Before You Pitch** – Follow, comment, and interact with brands before reaching out.

4. **Craft an Irresistible Pitch** – Highlight what makes you a valuable brand partner.

5. **Leverage Your Brand Deal for Future Opportunities** – Use successful collaborations to attract more deals.

What's Next?

At this stage, you've built a recognizable brand, mastered storytelling, expanded your reach on social media, and learned how to leverage strategic partnerships. But **a successful brand isn't just about getting attention—it's about keeping it.**

The most powerful personal brands don't just attract followers; they create **devoted, lifelong fans** who buy from them over and over again. This kind of **brand loyalty isn't accidental—it's intentional.**

Think about:

→ **Taylor Swift & The Swifties** – A fanbase so dedicated that they crash ticketing sites and fuel billion-dollar tours.

→ **Dwayne "The Rock" Johnson** – His audience follows him from wrestling to movies to tequila brands, proving that loyalty can extend across industries.

→ **Oprah Winfrey** – Decades later, she still has an audience that trusts her book recommendations, product endorsements, and personal insights.

What do these celebrities have in common? They **build emotional connections with their audience**, foster community, and make their fans feel like they're part of something bigger.

In Chapter 6, we'll dive into The Celebrity Marketing Playbook – How A-List Stars Build Massive Brand Loyalty.

You'll discover:

- How to turn customers into raving fans who promote your brand for free.

- The psychology behind brand loyalty and how to apply it to your business.

- How to create a movement, not just a product or service.

If you want your brand to thrive long-term, it's not just about sales— **it's about building relationships, trust, and a community that stands behind you. Let's get started!**

CHAPTER 6

The Celebrity Marketing Playbook – How A-List Stars Build Massive Brand Loyalty

Why Brand Loyalty is the Ultimate Competitive Advantage

In today's world, **attention is fleeting, and competition is fierce.** Consumers are bombarded with options, yet certain brands—especially those tied to celebrities—command unwavering loyalty.

Look at **Taylor Swift and Beyoncé**. Their fans don't just like them; they're devoted to them. Swifties and the BeyHive **support their albums, buy their merchandise, and promote their brands endlessly**. That kind of loyalty isn't accidental—it's **strategic brand-building**.

Loyalty isn't just for celebrities. Entrepreneurs and business owners can use the **same branding tactics** to create a following of **engaged, repeat customers who trust and advocate for them.** If you want

raving fans instead of one-time buyers, you need to master the art of brand loyalty.

"If people believe they share values with a company, they will stay loyal to the brand." – Howard Schultz (CEO, Starbucks)

The Biggest Brand Loyalty Mistakes That Kill Customer Retention

Many businesses focus **only on acquiring new customers** instead of nurturing the ones they already have. The problem? **Without loyalty, customers come and go—and so does your revenue.**

The Most Common Mistakes That Hurt Brand Loyalty

1. **Ignoring Your Audience After the First Sale** – If you disappear after someone buys, they won't stick around.

2. **Lack of Personal Connection** – Brands that feel **cold or transactional** fail to build real relationships.

3. **No Community Engagement** – The best brands **foster a sense of belonging.**

4. **Inconsistency in Branding** – Constantly changing your messaging confuses your audience.

5. **Overlooking Exclusivity & VIP Experiences** – People love feeling **special and part of an elite group.**

Successful celebrity brands **don't just sell—they create emotional experiences** that make people feel connected.

The Celebrity Brand Loyalty Formula – 5 Key Strategies

Create a Personal Connection (Make Your Audience Feel Seen & Heard)

The most powerful brands **build deep emotional connections with their audience.** Celebrities do this by making fans **feel valued and understood.**

Taylor Swift is a **master at this**. She randomly surprises fans with gifts, sends personalized messages, and engages with them on social media. As a result, Swifties feel like they have a real relationship with her.

How you can apply this:

- **Respond to customer messages, comments, and DMs.**
- **Feature customer stories and testimonials on your platforms.**
- **Personalize the customer experience** (emails, thank-you notes, exclusive access).

If people feel like they matter to you, they'll stick around for life.

2. Build a Community, Not Just a Customer Base

Celebrities **don't just attract fans—they build communities**. Beyoncé's BeyHive, Rihanna's Navy, and the Kardashian fanbase are **more than followers; they're tribes.**

Why does this matter? **People crave belonging.** When your brand makes them feel like part of something bigger, **they will stay engaged and loyal.**

How to build brand community:

- **Create an exclusive Facebook or Discord group** for your audience.

- **Encourage user-generated content (UGC).** Have customers share their experiences with your brand.

- **Host in-person or virtual meetups** to strengthen relationships.

When people feel like they belong to a **movement, not just a brand**, they become lifelong supporters.

3. Consistency Builds Trust & Loyalty

The most loyal fan bases form around brands that are **consistent**.

Think about McDonald's. No matter where you go, a **Big Mac tastes the same**. That **predictability creates trust**, which leads to **repeat customers**.

Beyoncé has kept her brand consistent for **decades**. Whether she's releasing music, launching Ivy Park, or doing business deals, her brand pillars—excellence, empowerment, and privacy—never change.

How to implement this:

- **Maintain a consistent brand voice across platforms.**

- Stick to your brand values and messaging.
- Deliver a high-quality experience every time.

When people know what to expect from your brand, **they will keep coming back.**

4. Reward Loyalty (People Love Feeling Like VIPs)

Exclusivity fuels brand loyalty. Celebrities create **VIP experiences** to keep their audience engaged.

Look at **Rihanna's Savage X Fenty VIP program**. Members get **exclusive products, special discounts, and early access** to new drops—giving them a reason to stay loyal.

How to incorporate exclusivity into your brand:

- Offer **VIP perks** (early access to products, exclusive content, or bonus services).
- Create a **rewards program** that incentivizes repeat business.
- Host **exclusive events or giveaways** to keep customers engaged.

When people feel like insiders, they'll stay committed to your brand.

5. Turn Customers Into Brand Advocates

The most powerful marketing tool? **Word-of-mouth.**

Celebrity brands thrive on **fan-driven marketing**. Fans **promote their idols for free** by sharing content, posting reviews, and bringing in new supporters.

Kim Kardashian **leveraged fan engagement to dominate the beauty and fashion industries**. Instead of spending millions on ads, she lets her audience market for her.

How to turn customers into brand advocates:

- Encourage customers to share reviews and testimonials.
- Create a referral program with incentives for sharing your brand.
- Feature user-generated content (UGC) on your social media.

Your most loyal customers will **happily market your brand for free— if you make them feel valued.**

Action Steps - Build a Loyal Fan Base for Your Brand

Want to create **superfans who stick with your brand for years?** Follow these steps:

1. **Engage with your audience daily** - Respond to comments, share user content, and show appreciation.

2. **Foster a sense of community** - Create spaces where your audience can connect.

3. **Stay consistent in your brand messaging and experience** - Trust builds loyalty.

4. **Offer VIP experiences & loyalty perks** – Make customers feel exclusive.

5. **Turn customers into brand advocates** – Encourage them to promote your brand.

What's Next?

Building a brand is one thing, but **creating a movement**—one that people feel connected to, rally behind, and actively promote—is what separates **good brands from legendary ones.**

The biggest celebrities **don't just have followers—they have communities**. These communities don't just consume their content or buy their products; they **identify with their brand, spread their message, and feel emotionally invested in their success.**

Think about:

→ **Beyoncé's Beyhive** – More than just fans, they defend her brand, amplify her releases, and create viral moments that extend her influence beyond music.

→ **Taylor Swift's Swifties** – A fanbase so powerful that they influence the music industry, break records, and even impact local economies.

→ **Kai Cenat's Streaming Empire** – A content creator who built a massive, engaged audience that follows him across platforms, drives viral trends, and fuels his success.

These celebrities didn't just attract fans; they activated them through a combination of consistent engagement, brand storytelling, and emotional connection.

In Chapter 7, we'll explore How Celebrities Build Massive Fan Bases (And How You Can Too).

You'll learn:

- How to foster deep engagement that keeps people coming back.

- How to turn casual followers into brand evangelists who promote your brand for free.

- The step-by-step formula for building a loyal community that sticks with you for the long haul.

Your brand isn't just about what you sell—it's about the **tribe you create**. If you want to grow your influence and make a lasting impact, **it's time to build your movement.**

CHAPTER 7

How Celebrities Build Massive Fan Bases (And How You Can Too)

The Secret to Turning Followers Into Devoted Fans

A strong fan base isn't built overnight—it's **cultivated through connection, engagement, and consistency**. The most successful celebrities don't just have followers; they have **communities of loyal supporters** who buy their products, promote their projects, and defend their brands.

Think about **Prince, Shonda Rhimes, and Steve Harvey**—their audiences aren't just casual fans; they are deeply invested in their brands and everything they create.

Prince cultivated a fiercely loyal following through his artistry, mystery, and dedication to his craft—so much so that even after his passing, his legacy and music continue to inspire generations.

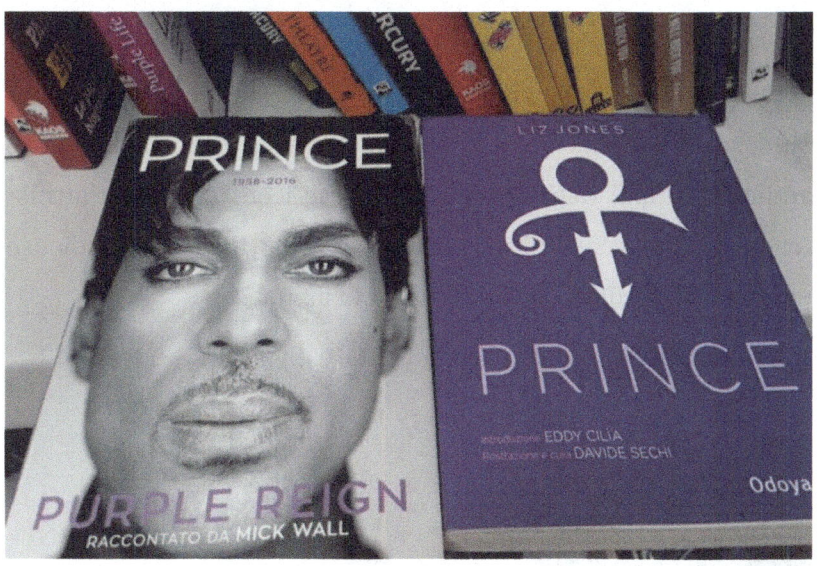

Shonda Rhimes built a storytelling empire that keeps audiences captivated year after year, with fans so dedicated that they create online communities, dissect her shows, and follow her every project.

Steve Harvey has mastered the art of reinvention, earning trust across multiple industries—whether in comedy, television, or personal development—because his audience connects with his authenticity and values his advice. These icons didn't just attract followers; they created movements, proving that deep audience engagement leads to lasting impact and influence.

What's the secret? They don't just entertain or sell—they create emotional connections. And that's exactly what you need to do to transform your audience from passive spectators into loyal, engaged super fans.

> *"A true fan isn't just a customer—they're an advocate who shares your brand with the world."*

The Biggest Mistakes That Prevent You From Growing a Loyal Audience

Many entrepreneurs and influencers focus too much on **gaining new followers** instead of **deepening their relationships with existing ones**. The result? Their audience feels **disconnected, uninvested, and quick to move on.**

The Most Common Mistakes That Kill Fan Engagement

1. **Focusing Too Much on Selling** – Fans want connection, not constant promotions.

2. **Lack of Consistency** – If you disappear for weeks at a time, your audience forgets about you.

3. **Ignoring Engagement** – Not responding to comments, messages, or fan contributions makes people feel unimportant.

4. **No Clear Brand Personality** – If you aren't distinct, you won't stand out.

5. **Not Giving Fans a Reason to Stay** – What's the incentive for your audience to stick around?

The biggest celebrities and influencers don't just post and disappear—they **foster relationships** that keep their audience engaged.

The Celebrity Blueprint for Building a Devoted Fan Base

1. Be Consistently Present & Show Up for Your Audience

The biggest mistake you can make? **Inconsistency.** Celebrities **stay visible year-round**, whether they have a project to promote or not.

Take Megan Thee Stallion, for example. Even when she's not releasing new music, she keeps her audience engaged through social media by sharing workout routines, beauty content, behind-the-scenes footage, and personal moments. She connects with fans authentically, whether through TikTok dance challenges, livestreams, or collaborations with brands like Nike and Revlon. By maintaining a strong presence and engaging directly with her community, she ensures that her brand stays top-of-mind year-round.

How to Apply This:

- → **Engage consistently** – Use Instagram, TikTok, and Twitter to interact with your audience beyond your main product or service.

- → **Show different sides of your brand** – Share personal insights, behind-the-scenes moments, or lifestyle content that resonates with your followers.

- → **Leverage trends & collaborations** – Jump on viral trends, collaborate with other influencers, and keep your audience involved in your journey.

Even when you're not launching something, stay engaged.

2. Make Your Audience Feel Like They Know You

Fans feel **connected to celebrities** who share their **real lives and personalities**. KeKe Palmer thrives because she doesn't just post polished content—**she's herself.** She shares her humor, **her struggles, and her wins, making her audience feel like friends, not just fans.**

How to apply this:

- **Share behind-the-scenes** content to make people feel included.

- **Use storytelling in your captions, videos, and interviews.**

- Let your audience see different sides of you—humor, vulnerability, wisdom.

3. Engage With Your Fans (It's a Two-Way Relationship)

Fans stick around **when they feel valued**. Michael Jackson was known for **personally engaging with fans, remembering their names, and making them feel special**. The biggest online influencers **respond to comments, DMs, and even surprise their followers with shoutouts**.

How to apply this:

- **Reply to comments and messages—don't just post and leave.**

- **Acknowledge loyal supporters by resharing their content or mentioning them in your posts.**

- **Host live Q&As, fan shoutouts, and exclusive content for engaged followers.**

4. Give Your Audience a Name & Identity

The most powerful fan bases **have names and a sense of community**.

- Beyoncé has the **BeyHive**.

- Lady Gaga has **Little Monsters**.

- Nicki Minaj has the **Barbz**.

Why does this matter? **When people feel like they belong to a movement, they stay loyal.**

How to apply this:

- **Create a name for your community.** It makes people feel included.
- **Encourage inside jokes, branded hashtags, or shared values within your group.**
- **Host events, livestreams, or meetups that strengthen the community.**

5. Turn Your Fans Into Brand Ambassadors

The most engaged fan bases don't just **consume content—they promote it.** Oprah's audience **doesn't just watch her show; they buy everything she recommends.** Michael Jackson's fans **didn't just listen to his music; they spread his influence worldwide.**

How to apply this:

- **Encourage user-generated content** (Ask fans to tag you in their posts).

- **Create a referral or loyalty program** to reward engaged followers.

- **Give fans incentives to share your content** (Exclusive access, giveaways, or shoutouts).

When your audience **feels like they're part of your success, they will naturally promote you.**

Action Steps – Grow a Devoted Fan Base Like a Celebrity

If you want to create loyal fans instead of passive followers, take these steps:

1. **Be Consistently Active** – Show up online regularly and stay engaged.

2. **Share Personal Stories & Behind-the-Scenes Moments** – Make your audience feel connected.

3. **Engage With Your Fans** – Reply to comments, messages, and shoutout your supporters.

4. **Give Your Audience an Identity** – Create a sense of community and belonging.

5. **Turn Your Fans Into Ambassadors** – Reward them for supporting and promoting your brand.

What's Next?

By now, you've learned how to grow your audience, build a loyal fan base, and leverage social media like a celebrity. But here's a challenge that every personal brand faces—how do you stay authentic while also maintaining a polished, professional image?

In today's digital world, audiences crave authenticity, but they're also drawn to aspirational brands that feel refined and well-curated. The most successful celebrities and entrepreneurs master the balance between being relatable and aspirational—sharing personal moments while still controlling their narrative.

Think about:

- → **Cardi B** – She's completely unfiltered and real on social media, but when it comes to her music and business ventures, everything is intentional and strategically curated.

- → **Kris Jenner & the Kardashian-Jenner Empire** – They make their lives seem open-book, but every piece of content is carefully planned to fit their branding.

→ **Jennifer Lopez** – She shares glimpses of her personal life but always presents herself as the ultimate professional and powerhouse performer.

These stars don't just post randomly—they strategically decide what to share, how to share it, and when to engage with their audience.

In Chapter 8, we'll explore Authenticity vs. Curation – How Celebrities Balance Realness and Perfection in Branding.

You'll learn:

- Why authenticity is key to building trust—but why curation is just as important.

- How to strategically share personal moments without oversharing.

- How to control your narrative while still being relatable and engaging.

If you've ever wondered **how much is too much to share** or struggled with **making your brand feel polished while staying real**, this chapter will give you the blueprint. Let's dive in!

CHAPTER 8

Authenticity vs. Curation – How Celebrities Balance Realness and Perfection in Branding

The Fine Line Between Being Real and Being Polished

In today's digital world, people crave **authenticity**—but they also expect a level of **polish and professionalism**. The most successful celebrities have mastered this delicate balance, appearing **relatable yet aspirational, personal yet controlled**. They share enough of their lives to keep audiences engaged but **never lose control of their narrative**.

Think about **Michelle Obama, Gordon Ramsay, and Jennifer Hudson**—three globally recognized figures from different industries, yet each has perfected the **art of authenticity** without overexposure.

→ **Michelle Obama** – She connects deeply with audiences by sharing personal stories about her upbringing, motherhood, and career challenges. Her books and speeches make her feel approachable, but she carefully controls what she reveals, ensuring her brand remains rooted in inspiration, leadership, and empowerment.

→ **Jennifer Hudson** – She is known for her powerhouse vocals and inspiring rags-to-riches story, openly sharing her journey from American Idol contestant to award-winning singer and actress. Her authenticity shines through as she discusses her personal triumphs, faith, and deep connection to her roots. However, she carefully curates her public persona, ensuring that her brand remains elegant, empowering, and focused on resilience and success. Whether she's hosting her talk show, performing on stage, or launching new projects, she maintains a balance between relatability and professionalism, making her an aspirational yet deeply genuine figure.

→ **Gordon Ramsay** – He's known for his fiery, no-nonsense attitude in the kitchen, but his social media presence—full of cooking videos, humor, and family moments—adds a softer, more relatable side to his brand. Even with his unscripted persona, he carefully curates his public image to reinforce his status as an elite chef and entrepreneur.

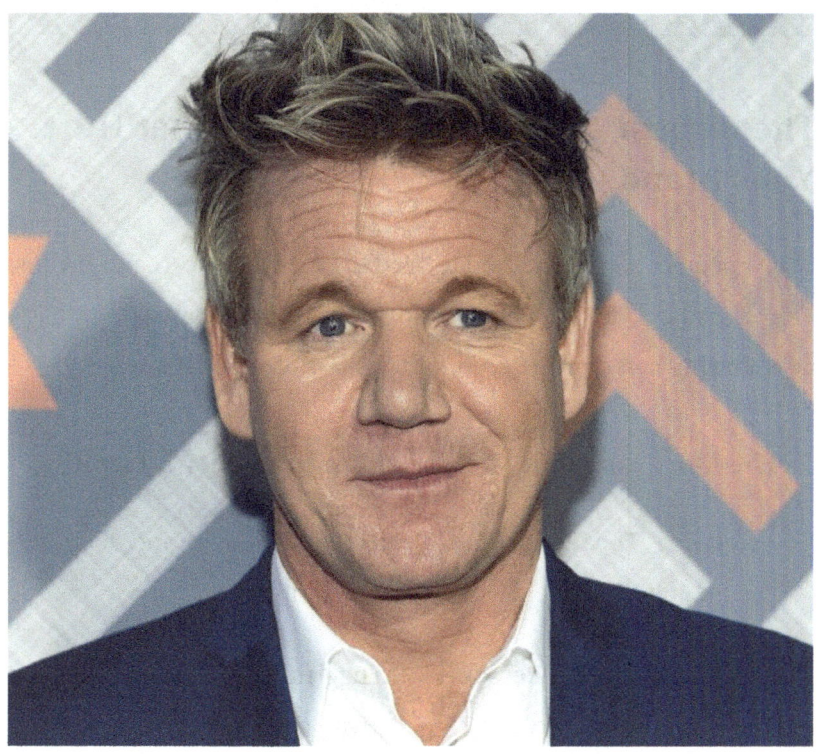

The Secret to Their Success?

They craft a personal brand that **feels real, engaging, and transparent**—but every move is intentional. They control what they share, ensuring that their public persona aligns with their larger mission, message, and business goals. **This is the key to building a powerful brand that connects with audiences while maintaining influence, credibility, and longevity.**

"Your audience wants the real you—but they also want the best version of you."

The Biggest Authenticity Mistakes That Hurt Your Brand

Many people misunderstand what **being authentic** really means. They assume it means **sharing everything**—but in reality, **oversharing can damage credibility and professionalism.**

The Most Common Mistakes in Authenticity & Curation

1. **Being Too Polished & Perfect** – If your brand feels too "manufactured," people won't trust it.

2. **Oversharing Personal Struggles** – Transparency is powerful, but too much negativity can push people away.

3. **Ignoring Your Audience's Expectations** – If people expect professionalism from you, don't suddenly go unfiltered.

4. **Being Inconsistent** – Switching between extreme authenticity and high curation confuses your audience.

5. **Not Understanding Boundaries** – Some things should stay private. Sharing too much can hurt your credibility.

The best personal brands **find the balance between real and refined.**

How Celebrities Balance Authenticity and Curation

They Share Real Stories, But They Control the Narrative

Authenticity doesn't mean sharing **everything**. It means sharing the **right things in the right way.**

Taylor Swift shares stories about heartbreak in her music, but she never reveals **every detail of her personal relationships**. Instead, she keeps fans engaged by letting them **interpret the story themselves.**

How to apply this:

- Share **personal stories** that reinforce your brand message.

- Avoid **negative or reactive posts** that could damage your reputation.

- Keep some aspects of your life **private to maintain professionalism.**

2. They Let Their Personality Shine Without Losing Professionalism

Gayle King is a great example of this. As a journalist and co-host of CBS Mornings, she is known for her warm, engaging, and down-to-earth personality. She openly shares aspects of her life, from her friendship with Oprah to personal experiences that make her relatable. However, she carefully maintains her credibility as a journalist, ensuring that her authenticity never overshadows her professionalism. Whether she's conducting hard-hitting interviews or sharing candid moments on social media, Gayle strikes the perfect balance between **realness and refinement**, making her one of the most trusted and respected voices in media.

How to Apply This:

→ Engage your audience with personal storytelling while maintaining professionalism.

→ Be relatable, but ensure your content aligns with your brand and industry standards.

→ Control your narrative—share enough to connect, but never at the expense of credibility.

3. They Use Social Media to Build Real Connections—But With Strategy

DJ Khaled is a master of using social media to engage with his audience in an authentic yet strategic way. Whether he's sharing motivational messages, behind-the-scenes glimpses of his music career, or moments with his family, everything he posts reinforces his brand of **positivity, hustle, and success**. His larger-than-life personality makes him feel accessible, but every post serves a purpose—whether it's promoting a new project, strengthening partnerships, or building deeper connections with fans.

How to Apply This:

→ **Engage with your audience genuinely**—respond to comments, interact with followers, and let them feel like part of your journey.

→ **Be intentional about what you share**—before posting, ask yourself, "Does this align with my brand and business goals?"

→ **Use real moments to build trust**—but always maintain control over your narrative to ensure your message stays on-brand.

4. They Show Their Process, Not Just the Final Product

People love seeing behind the scenes. They don't just want the polished final result—they want the journey.

LeBron James is a perfect example of this. His Strive for Greatness mentality isn't just a slogan—it's something he lives and documents daily. Whether he's posting intense gym workouts, behind-the-scenes moments from game prep, or film study breakdowns, LeBron gives his audience a firsthand look at the work that goes into being one of the greatest athletes of all time. He doesn't just show the wins—he **shares the grind, discipline, and setbacks**, making his success feel even more inspiring.

How to Apply This:

- → **Document, don't just create**—share behind-the-scenes moments that show your work in action.

- → **Be real about the struggles and wins**—people relate more to the journey than just the success.

- → **Let your audience grow with you**—when they see your evolution, they feel personally invested in your brand.

5. They Set Boundaries and Stay in Control

Authenticity doesn't mean **giving everyone access to everything**. Celebrities set **firm boundaries** about what's public and what's private.

For example, Beyoncé keeps her personal life **extremely private**, only sharing what aligns with her brand. Yet, she remains **one of the most admired and followed celebrities in the world**.

How to apply this:

- Decide **what you will and won't share.** Stick to it.

- Keep some personal details private to **maintain mystique.**

- Control your public image, **instead of letting others control it for you.**

Action Steps - Master the Art of Authenticity & Curation

If you want to **balance realness with a polished brand image,** follow these steps:

1. **Decide what personal stories align with your brand**—share what reinforces your message.

2. **Let your personality shine, but maintain professionalism**—be real, not reckless.

3. **Use social media to connect, but with strategy**—engagement matters, but control the narrative.

4. **Show behind-the-scenes moments**—let people in, but on your terms.

5. **Set boundaries and protect your brand image**—share enough to be relatable, but keep private matters private.

What's Next?

Success isn't just about making an impact—it's about staying relevant. The most iconic celebrities aren't just famous; they

reinvent themselves to maintain longevity, influence, and cultural relevance. Whether it's through strategic career shifts, brand evolution, or tapping into new audiences, reinvention is a key factor in staying at the top.

In **Chapter 9, we'll explore The Power of Personal Reinvention – How Celebrities Stay Relevant for Decades**. You'll learn how stars like Madonna, Will Smith, and Robert Downey Jr. have reinvented **themselves time and time again** to maintain their status as household names.

You'll discover:

- **How to pivot your brand without losing your core audience.**

- **The key to adapting to industry shifts, new trends, and emerging platforms.**

- **How reinvention can unlock new revenue streams and opportunities.**

The world moves fast, and standing still is not an option. **By learning the strategies of the biggest stars, you'll be equipped to refresh, refine, and future-proof your personal brand.** Let's dive in!

CHAPTER 9

The Power of Personal Reinvention – How Celebrities Stay Relevant for Decades

Why Reinvention is the Key to Longevity in Your Brand

The biggest mistake people make in branding? **They stay the same for too long.**

The world moves fast—**trends shift, audiences evolve, and industries change.** The brands and public figures that stand the test of time are the ones who **know how to reinvent themselves without losing their core identity.**

Look at Snoop Dogg, Tyra Banks, and Whoopi Goldberg.

→ **Snoop Dogg** has evolved far beyond his hip-hop roots, building a brand empire that includes television, film, cannabis, esports, and even a cooking show with Martha Stewart. He has mastered the art of reinvention by staying true to his persona while expanding into unexpected industries, proving that adaptability is key to longevity.

→ **Tyra Banks** went from supermodel to TV personality, business mogul, and educator. After dominating the fashion world, she built America's Next Top Model, became a talk show host, launched beauty brands, and even taught a personal branding course at Stanford. Her ability to pivot and remain relevant in multiple industries highlights the power of reinvention.

→ **Whoopi Goldberg** is an EGOT-winning legend who has seamlessly transitioned between acting, comedy, hosting, and producing. From The Color Purple to Sister Act to The View, she has continuously evolved her brand, staying relevant in entertainment, activism, and media. Her ability to reinvent herself across decades proves that versatility is one of the strongest assets in building a lasting career.

These icons prove that reinvention is about embracing new opportunities, diversifying your brand, and staying ahead of industry shifts—while remaining authentic to your core identity.

"Reinvention isn't about changing who you are—it's about staying ahead of the curve while staying true to your essence."

The Biggest Reinvention Mistakes That Kill a Brand

Many people resist change because they're afraid of losing their identity. Others reinvent themselves too drastically, confusing their audience and damaging their credibility.

The Most Common Mistakes in Reinvention

1. **Waiting Too Long to Evolve** – If you wait until your brand is fading, it may be too late.

2. **Changing Too Drastically, Too Fast** – Reinvention should feel natural, not forced.

3. **Ignoring Your Audience's Needs** – If your audience no longer resonates with your brand, they will leave.

4. **Forgetting Core Brand Values** – The best reinventions keep a brand's essence intact.

5. **Not Leveraging New Platforms or Trends** – If you refuse to adapt, you will fall behind.

Reinvention is a **strategy, not a reaction.** The best brands plan for change **before it becomes necessary.**

The Celebrity Formula for Staying Relevant

1. Read the Cultural Landscape and Anticipate Change

The most successful celebrities stay ahead of trends, rather than reacting to them.

50 Cent mastered this strategy by recognizing early on that success in the music industry alone wasn't enough. After dominating rap in the early 2000s, he saw the increasing importance of brand partnerships and business ventures. Instead of just endorsing products, he secured an equity deal with Vitaminwater, which led to a reported **$100 million payout when the brand was sold to Coca-Cola.** He then expanded into television with Power, capitalizing on the rise of streaming and premium cable dramas, further cementing his influence beyond music.

How to Apply This:

- → **Stay ahead of industry shifts**—don't just react to trends; be the one setting them.

- → **Look for expansion opportunities**—align your brand with new industries that fit your audience.

- → **Leverage your expertise and influence**—use your platform to create long-term business success, not just short-term wins.

By reading the cultural landscape and anticipating change, **50 Cent evolved from a rap star into a business mogul, proving that true influence comes from adaptability and strategic reinvention.**

2. Keep Your Core Identity, but Update Your Messaging

Reinvention doesn't mean changing who you are—it means adapting your message to stay relevant while staying true to your core values.

Oprah Winfrey is a master of this. She started as a daytime talk show host, becoming one of the most influential media figures of all time. But when The Oprah Winfrey Show ended, she didn't just disappear—she evolved. She launched OWN (Oprah Winfrey Network), produced award-winning content, expanded her brand into wellness, spirituality, and book curation, and leveraged streaming platforms like Apple TV+ to reach new audiences. Despite all these shifts, her core identity remains the same—**a storyteller and mentor who empowers people through meaningful conversations and self-improvement.**

How to Apply This:

- → **Adapt your message to new platforms—don't rely on one medium to carry your brand forever.**

- → **Expand into new opportunities while staying true to your core mission.**

- → **Evolve with your audience—grow with them while maintaining the authenticity that made them connect with you in the first place.**

By continuously updating her approach while keeping her brand rooted in personal growth and empowerment, **Oprah remains a dominant force in media and business decades after her talk show ended.**

3. Expand Into New Platforms and Industries

Celebrities don't limit themselves to one space. They diversify and enter new industries, ensuring their brand remains relevant across different audiences.

Michael Strahan transitioned from an NFL superstar to a media powerhouse. After retiring from football, he became a successful TV personality, co-hosting Good Morning America, leading Fox NFL Sunday, and even launching his own men's fashion line at JCPenney. His ability to pivot into broadcasting and business proves that expanding into new industries can open up long-term career success.

Queen Latifah went from hip-hop pioneer to award-winning actress, producer, and businesswoman. She started as a rapper, then moved into TV and film, starring in Living Single and major Hollywood films like Chicago. She later expanded into production with Flavor Unit Entertainment, creating opportunities behind the scenes. Her ability to move seamlessly across industries while maintaining her core brand of empowerment and confidence has made her a cultural icon.

How to Apply This:

→ **Identify new platforms where your brand can grow**—your expertise may translate into multiple industries.

→ **Look for partnerships and collaborations** that introduce you to new audiences.

→ **Be open to evolving**—expanding your expertise into new areas can unlock new revenue streams and opportunities.

By stepping outside of their original careers and embracing new industries, **Michael Strahan and Queen Latifah have built long-lasting brands that continue to evolve and expand.**

4. Stay Visible and Engaged with Your Audience

If people stop hearing about you, they stop thinking about you. Celebrities who stay relevant stay active, ensuring they remain part of the cultural conversation.

Will Smith is a master of this. After decades as a Hollywood A-lister, he didn't just rely on his past success—he actively reinvented his connection with audiences. When traditional media roles slowed down, he took matters into his own hands, launching a **hugely successful YouTube channel**, where he shared behind-the-scenes footage, personal challenges, and entertaining stunts. He leveraged social media, producing viral content on Instagram and TikTok, engaging younger fans who might not have grown up watching The Fresh Prince of Bel-Air. His willingness to embrace new platforms kept him culturally relevant, proving that staying engaged with audiences is key to longevity.

How to Apply This:

→ **Show up consistently on social media and media platforms**—staying visible keeps your brand top-of-mind.

→ **Keep your brand active even between major projects**—share behind-the-scenes content, personal updates, or industry insights.

→ **Find new ways to engage younger or different audiences**—whether it's through new platforms, collaborations, or evolving content styles.

Will Smith proves that visibility and engagement are essential for long-term relevance—because the more present you are, the more people will continue to connect with your brand.

5. Own Your Reinvention Story

One of the biggest reinvention pitfalls? **Letting the narrative control you instead of controlling the narrative.** The most successful celebrities and entrepreneurs don't just evolve behind the scenes—they shape the story of their transformation and present it with confidence.

When Martha Stewart went to prison, she could have faded away, but instead, she embraced the story and used it to reintroduce herself. She didn't hide from the experience—she leaned into it, proving that resilience and reinvention go hand in hand. She re-emerged stronger, expanding her brand, collaborating with unexpected figures like Snoop Dogg, and maintaining her status as a trusted lifestyle icon. Instead of allowing the media to define her downfall, she **took ownership of her story and controlled the way the world perceived her comeback.**

The same principle applies to **anyone undergoing a career pivot, brand shift, or public challenge**—the key to reinvention is not just evolving but communicating that evolution in a way that reinforces **growth, strength, and purpose.**

How to Apply This:

- → **If your brand is shifting, communicate that story with confidence**—people respect leaders who own their transformations.

- → **Be transparent about why you're evolving and what it means for your audience**—clarity builds trust and keeps people engaged in your journey.

- → **Position your reinvention as growth, not failure**—every pivot is an opportunity to expand your influence, reach new audiences, and increase your value.

By owning your reinvention story and taking control of the narrative, you don't just stay relevant—you build an even stronger, more resilient brand.

Action Steps – Successfully Reinvent Your Brand Without Losing Your Audience

If you want to **stay relevant, evolve strategically** with these steps:

1. **Analyze Your Industry & Trends** – Stay ahead of changes before they impact your brand.

2. **Refine Your Brand Identity** – Keep your core values but update your messaging.

3. **Expand Your Brand Presence** – Explore new industries, platforms, and collaborations.

4. **Stay Consistently Visible** – Keep engaging with your audience to maintain relevance.

5. **Control Your Reinvention Story** – Position your evolution as a powerful next step, not a desperate change.

What's Next?

Building a powerful brand is only the beginning—the **real success comes from turning that brand into long-term wealth.** The most successful celebrities don't just rely on their original careers; they create multiple revenue streams that **keep their influence (and income) growing for decades.**

In **Chapter 10, we'll explore The Celebrity Business Empire – How to Turn Your Personal Brand Into Multiple Streams of Income.** You'll learn how A-list stars like **Rihanna, Snoop Dogg, and Jessica Alba** have built **business empires that extend far beyond music, movies, or TV**—and how their strategies can apply to you.

You'll discover:

- **The key to leveraging your personal brand to create multiple revenue streams.**

- **How to transition from a solo brand to a scalable business.**

- **The most profitable industries and business models celebrities use to sustain long-term success.**

Your personal brand is an asset. Now, it's time to learn how to monetize it in ways that create lasting success, security, and financial freedom. Let's dive in!

CHAPTER 10

The Celebrity Business Empire – How to Turn Your Personal Brand Into Multiple Streams of Income

Why Every Strong Personal Brand Needs Multiple Income Streams

Building a personal brand is powerful—but **turning that brand into a business empire is where true wealth is created.**

The most successful entrepreneurs, doctors, fitness trainers, and financial experts don't rely on just one revenue source. They **diversify, invest, and expand their brand across multiple industries**, ensuring they create wealth that lasts long after their initial success.

Let's look at how some of the most recognizable industry leaders have leveraged their personal brands into **multiple streams of income and multi-million-dollar business empires:**

→ **Dr. Mark Hyman** – What started as a medical practice turned into a **global health brand**. As one of the leading voices in functional medicine, he has monetized his expertise by **writing best-selling books** (Young Forever, Food Fix), launching **digital health programs**, creating a **line of supplements and wellness products**, and building **The UltraWellness Center**, where people can receive high-end personalized care. His **marketing funnel strategically attracts patients and consumers**, guiding them from free educational content to paid wellness programs and products.

→ **Shaun T** – Once a fitness trainer, Shaun T transformed his workouts into a **multi-platform fitness empire**. His partnership with **Beachbody** turned **Insanity** and **T25** into some of the most successful home workout programs ever. He has since expanded into **fitness coaching, motivational speaking, merchandise, books, live fitness events, and digital workout subscriptions**. His personal brand allows him to sell to millions of people globally, generating revenue long after his initial workouts were filmed.

→ **Suze Orman** – Known as one of the most trusted voices in personal finance, Suze Orman has built a **financial education empire** by monetizing her expertise across **books, TV shows, financial coaching programs, and online courses**. She doesn't just give advice—she sells **financial planning tools,**

memberships, and training programs that help people manage money effectively. Her **digital content and automated sales funnels** allow her to generate revenue even when she's not actively teaching or speaking.

These experts **didn't just stick to their original career path**—they built businesses that generate revenue in multiple ways:

- **Books & Digital Products** – Turning knowledge into monetizable assets.

- **Coaching & Courses** – Scaling their expertise to help more people.

- **Brand Partnerships & Licensing** – Aligning with trusted brands to expand their influence.

- **Subscription Models & Memberships** – Creating ongoing, passive income.

- **Speaking Engagements & Events** – Positioning themselves as high-paid industry leaders.

The key to long-term success? **Building a business that works for you—even when you're not actively working.**

If you want to grow a powerful, sustainable brand, **you need to think beyond one revenue stream and start building a business empire that keeps working for you.**

> "Your brand is the foundation, but multiple income streams are the empire."

The Biggest Mistakes That Keep Entrepreneurs Stuck in One Income Stream

Many personal brands struggle to scale because **they focus only on their main business or profession and never branch out.**

The Most Common Mistakes That Limit Business Growth

1. **Relying on One Source of Income** – If that revenue stream disappears, so does your business.

2. **Not Leveraging Brand Partnerships** – Brands are willing to pay you if your audience trusts you.

3. **Failing to Monetize Digital Products** – If you're not selling knowledge-based products, you're leaving money on the table.

4. **Ignoring Passive Income Opportunities** – If all your income requires your time, you'll always be working.

5. **Not Treating Their Brand Like a Business** – You are a brand—but you must operate like a company.

The good news? **Celebrities have a proven blueprint for brand monetization, and you can use it too.**

How Celebrities Monetize Their Personal Brands

1. Build a Profitable Product Line (Like Rihanna & Dr. Dre)

One of the fastest ways to **monetize your brand** is by creating a **physical or digital product.**

- Rihanna launched Fenty Beauty and disrupted the beauty industry.

- Dr. Dre created Beats by Dre, which became a multi-billion-dollar brand.
- Kim Kardashian built SKIMS, turning shapewear into a luxury product.

How to apply this:

→ Identify a **product or service your audience would love.**

→ Start with **digital products (e-books, courses, membership sites).**

→ If you create physical products, **focus on niche, high-demand items.**

2. Monetize Your Content & Influence (Like Tim Ferriss & Alex Cooper)

Your brand is an asset—and when leveraged correctly, it becomes a **powerful revenue-generating machine.** The most successful entrepreneurs don't just create content; they **strategically monetize their influence** across multiple platforms, turning their expertise into multiple income streams.

Tim Ferriss – Best-selling author of The 4-Hour Workweek and host of The Tim Ferriss Show, Tim turned his expertise into a **content-driven business empire.** He writes books, hosts a top-ranked podcast, publishes a newsletter, and creates exclusive content that attracts a dedicated audience. His brand generates revenue through **sponsorships, high-profile brand partnerships, online courses, affiliate marketing, and speaking engagements.** By consistently producing valuable content, he has built an audience that **trusts his recommendations, making sponsorships and product collaborations incredibly lucrative.**

Alex Cooper – Host of Call Her Daddy, she transformed her podcast from a viral sensation into a **$60 million Spotify-exclusive deal**. Beyond her contract, she **monetizes her influence through brand sponsorships, social media partnerships, and premium content on platforms like Instagram and TikTok**. She has expanded into media production with her company, Unwell, and with her massive influence, a book or exclusive newsletter could be the next step in monetizing her content ecosystem.

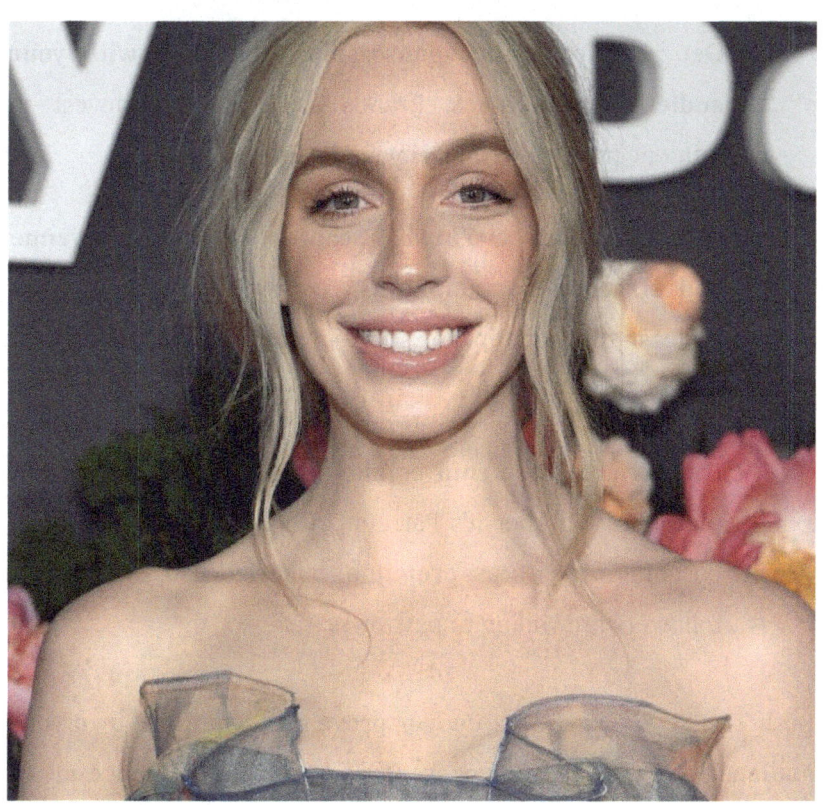

How to Apply This:

- → **Write a book that establishes your expertise and builds passive income.** Books not only position you as a thought leader but also generate revenue through direct sales, speaking engagements, and brand partnerships.

- → **Start a podcast or newsletter to engage your audience regularly.** These platforms create **consistent content touch-points** and can be monetized through ads, sponsorships, and premium subscriptions.

→ **Get paid for brand sponsorships that align with your audience and values.** Brands are willing to invest in influencers with strong, engaged communities.

→ **Monetize your social media & content through ad revenue and strategic partnerships.** Whether through YouTube, podcast sponsorships, or social media, leverage your reach for consistent income.

→ **Launch a membership community or exclusive content platform.** Whether it's Patreon, a digital course, or private coaching, create a **premium experience** that fans or followers are willing to pay for.

Both **Tim Ferriss and Alex Cooper prove that when you own your audience and control your content, you can turn influence into a powerful, multi-revenue business model that works for you.** Whether through **books, podcasts, newsletters, or digital platforms,** the key is creating **monetizable content that keeps your audience engaged and willing to invest in your expertise.**

3. Turn Your Expertise Into High-Ticket Services & Coaching

If people see you as an expert, they will pay for access to your knowledge. The most successful personal brands don't just share information—they package their expertise into high-ticket coaching, consulting, and exclusive experiences that command premium pricing.

Tony Robbins – Tony Robbins started his journey with personal development seminars and has since **built a billion-dollar empire** by offering **premium coaching, high-level business mentorship, and transformational live events.** Programs like **Unleash the Power Within and Business Mastery** draw thousands of attendees who pay significant fees for life-changing content. He also runs **Platinum Partnership**, a **high-ticket coaching program** that provides direct access to Robbins himself, further solidifying his position as one of the most successful coaches in the world. His business model proves that expertise, paired with exclusive access, can lead to substantial revenue.

Russell Brunson – The founder of **ClickFunnels**, Russell Brunson is another example of an entrepreneur who has turned his expertise into multiple high-revenue streams. Through his **book sales (like DotCom Secrets and Expert Secrets), online courses, live events, and coaching programs, he has built a multi-million-dollar business**. His **high-ticket coaching and funnel-building programs** allow entrepreneurs to learn directly from him, positioning him as a leader in the digital marketing space. He also launched **Funnel Hacking Live**, an event that attracts thousands of entrepreneurs to learn from his strategies, all while paying premium fees for in-person access.

How to Apply This:

- → **Offer consulting or high-ticket coaching.** Create personalized, exclusive programs that offer direct access to your expertise.

- → **Create a mastermind group or VIP community.** A **private membership group** or **elite coaching circle** can allow you to offer advanced training and networking at premium rates.

- → **Host virtual or in-person workshops.** Scale your knowledge through **workshops and live events**, turning your expertise into a valuable experience that people will pay for.

- → **Build a signature course or certification program.** Design **high-ticket courses** and **certification programs** that offer high-value content and enable clients to level up their businesses or skills.

The Key Takeaway:

By offering **exclusive coaching, high-ticket services, and expert-led content**, you can position yourself as an industry authority while **generating significant revenue**. Whether through **VIP mentorship, signature courses, or exclusive workshops**, leveraging your expertise and personal brand can create multiple streams of income and long-term success.

4. Invest in Businesses, Real Estate & Equity Deals

Invest Like a Celebrity – How the Wealthiest Stars Build Lasting Wealth

The wealthiest celebrities don't just earn money—**they invest in businesses that generate wealth long after their primary careers fade.** They understand that true financial freedom comes from **leveraging their earnings to own and grow assets.**

Jay-Z – One of the most business-savvy entertainers, Jay-Z invested in **Uber** early when it was valued at just **$300 million**. His stake reportedly grew to **tens of millions** as the company skyrocketed. Beyond that, he built **Roc Nation**, launched **Armand de Brignac Champagne**, and invested in **real estate and tech startups**, proving that investing outside of music is key to building generational wealth.

Shaquille O'Neal – The NBA legend turned entrepreneur has built an impressive **investment portfolio** that includes franchise ownership in brands like **Papa John's, Krispy Kreme, and Five Guys**, as well as investments in **Google and tech startups**. Shaq has mastered the art of using his personal brand to **partner with and invest in high-growth companies**, securing long-term financial success.

Dr. Deepak Chopra – A pioneer in integrative medicine and mindfulness, Chopra has built a multi-million-dollar business around wellness retreats, books, online courses, meditation apps, and partnerships with major brands like Fitbit and Oprah's wellness network. His investments in digital health and mindfulness platforms have helped him stay ahead in the wellness industry.

Ashton Kutcher – He turned his Hollywood success into a **powerful venture capital career**, co-founding **A-Grade Investments**. His firm made **early investments in Airbnb, Spotify, and Uber, turning relatively small stakes into millions in returns**. His ability to **identify high-growth startups** has made him one of the most successful celebrity investors in Silicon Valley.

How to Apply This:

→ **Set aside income to invest in businesses or startups.** Even small investments can grow into long-term wealth when placed in the right companies.

→ **Look for equity deals (get paid in ownership, not just cash).** Instead of taking one-time payments, negotiate equity in startups, brands, or projects that can provide long-term financial benefits.

→ **Consider real estate or digital asset investments for passive income.** From commercial properties to digital brands, investing in income-generating assets can secure long-term financial success.

The Key Takeaway:

Making money is great, but **investing that money wisely is how the wealthiest individuals sustain and multiply their wealth**. Whether it's **startups, franchises, real estate, or digital assets**, diversifying income streams and **owning pieces of high-growth businesses** is the real secret to long-term financial security.

5. License Your Name & Brand for Passive Income

When your brand carries influence, companies will pay for the right to use your name, image, or expertise—creating passive income streams that generate revenue long after the initial deal is signed. Celebrities, entrepreneurs, and industry leaders have leveraged licensing to earn millions without needing to create products themselves.

Michael Jordan & Air Jordan – One of the most **iconic athlete endorsements in history,** Jordan's deal with **Nike** transformed his brand into a **billion-dollar empire**. Instead of just taking a one-time paycheck, he negotiated a **royalty-based deal, earning a percentage of every sale.** The Air Jordan brand continues to generate **hundreds**

of millions annually, proving that licensing deals can create generational wealth.

George Foreman & The Foreman Grill – The former boxing champ didn't invent the grill—but he licensed his **name and brand power** to the product, earning over **$200 million** from royalties. Foreman didn't have to design, manufacture, or sell the grills himself—he simply licensed his name and let the company handle everything else.

Dr. Bill Dorfman & Zoom Whitening – A world-renowned cosmetic dentist, Dr. Dorfman built **Zoom Whitening**, one of the most popular professional teeth-whitening brands. Instead of keeping it within his practice, he licensed it to other dentists worldwide, creating **passive income through licensing fees** while expanding his influence in the industry.

Martha Stewart & Martha Stewart Living – She turned her expertise in homemaking and lifestyle branding into a licensing powerhouse, securing deals with retailers like Macy's, Home Depot, and Wayfair. These partnerships allow companies to sell products under her name, while she earns ongoing royalties without personally managing every product line.

How to Apply This:

- → **Negotiate brand deals that pay royalties.** Instead of just endorsing a product for a one-time fee, **negotiate a percentage of ongoing sales** for long-term income.

→ **License your brand for courses, content, or products.** If you're an expert, **companies may pay to license your methods, training, or digital content** under their brand.

→ **Turn your expertise into a franchise model.** If you've developed a successful method or service, **train others to use your system and collect licensing fees.**

The Key Takeaway:

The real power of branding isn't just in selling products—it's in **owning your intellectual property and getting paid for it over and over again.** Whether through **endorsement deals, training programs, or product licensing, finding ways to make money without actively working for every dollar is the ultimate wealth-building strategy.**

Action Steps – Turn Your Personal Brand Into an Empire

If you want to **expand your income beyond one revenue stream**, follow these steps:

1. Identify monetization opportunities that align with your brand.

2. Start with digital products, consulting, or a membership community.

3. Leverage brand partnerships & sponsorships to generate revenue.
4. Invest in businesses, real estate, or passive income opportunities.
5. Think like a business mogul, not just a personal brand.

What's Next?

The Final Chapter: Wrapping It All Together & Taking Action

Now that you have a **complete roadmap** for branding, influence, and monetization, it's time to take action.

In the final chapter, I'll show you **how to put these strategies into motion, refine your game plan, and start executing like a celebrity brand builder.**

CHAPTER 11

Wrapping It All Together & Taking Action Like a Celebrity Brand Builder

The Roadmap to Building a Powerful, Profitable Personal Brand

You've learned how the world's **biggest celebrities build influence, create brand loyalty, and turn their personal brands into thriving business empires.** Now, it's time to **put these strategies into action.**

The biggest difference between celebrities who dominate their industries and those who fade into the background? **Execution.**

The most successful personal brands—**Oprah, Rihanna, Kevin Hart, Dr. Dre, and Taylor Swift—don't just think about strategy. They implement it consistently.**

"Success isn't about talent alone—it's about strategy, consistency, and execution."

This final chapter is your **step-by-step action plan** to transform what you've learned into real-world results.

The Celebrity Brand Builder Blueprint – Your Next Steps

If you're serious about growing your brand, it's time to take focused, strategic action. Here's how to **apply everything you've learned**.

Step 1 – Define & Position Your Brand Identity

Your brand should be **instantly recognizable and deeply connected to your values.** Ask yourself:

- **What is your brand identity?** (Expert, entertainer, innovator, leader?)

- **What are your brand values?** (Luxury, empowerment, humor, expertise?)

- **How do you want your audience to describe you?**

If you don't define your personal brand, **the world will define it for you.** Take control of your narrative.

Step 2 – Create a Signature Look & Presence

First impressions matter. Your image should be **consistent and strategically designed** to align with your brand.

- Define your **visual style (colors, fashion, logos, photography aesthetic)**.
- Invest in **professional branding materials (website, headshots, content)**.
- Be recognizable across **every platform you use.**

Step 3 – Master Storytelling to Connect with Your Audience

The most powerful brands are built through **stories that resonate.**

- Craft your **brand story with a clear transformation.**
- Share personal experiences that **relate to your audience.**
- Use storytelling across **social media, interviews, and speaking engagements.**

If your audience **sees themselves in your story, they will support your brand.**

Step 4 – Build & Engage a Loyal Audience

Social media is your **megaphone**—use it wisely.

- Choose **3-5 content pillars** that align with your brand.
- Stay consistent with posting and engagement.
- Build a **real connection** with your audience (respond to comments, ask questions, go live).

Your **fans should feel like they are part of something bigger**. That's how celebrities build movements, not just audiences.

Step 5 – Monetize & Expand Your Brand Into Multiple Income Streams

To create long-term success, you must **think like a business**.

- Launch **digital products, courses, or memberships**.
- Secure **brand partnerships, sponsorships, or ambassador deals**.
- Explore **investments, licensing deals, and passive income opportunities**.

The wealthiest personal brands **don't rely on one revenue stream—they diversify**.

Step 6 - Reinvent & Evolve to Stay Relevant

If you're not growing, you're becoming irrelevant. The best brands evolve over time.

- Stay ahead of **industry trends and audience shifts.**
- Refresh your messaging **without losing your brand essence.**
- Be open to expanding your expertise into new areas.

Madonna and Martha Stewart **mastered reinvention.** If you want longevity, **so should you.**

Taking the Next Step - Where Do You Go From Here?

Now that you have the blueprint, it's time to take action.

Most people read, get inspired, and then do nothing. The ones who succeed are the ones who implement consistently, refine their strategy, and keep showing up. **Building a brand like a celebrity isn't about luck—it's about execution.**

Don't let this be another thing you "think about doing." The difference between those who stay stuck and those who elevate their brands is simple: **commitment and action.**

Here's What To Do Right Now: Your Immediate Action Plan

1. **Clarify your brand identity.** Define your mission, values, and unique positioning. Ask yourself: What do I want to be known for? Who is my audience? How can I stand out?

2. **Audit your online presence.** Look at your website, social media, and content strategy. Is your messaging clear? Does your brand image match your goals? If not, now is the time to refine it.

3. **Develop your monetization plan.** Identify ways to turn your brand into multiple income streams. Will you launch a book, course, coaching program, or a high-ticket offer?

4. **Increase your visibility.** Start positioning yourself for media features, collaborations, and brand partnerships. Build credibility by showing up where your audience is.

5. **Get expert guidance.** If you're ready to build a powerful, profitable personal brand, don't do it alone. Work with someone who knows how to fast-track your success.

Let's Work Together – Build Your Brand Like a Celebrity

If you're ready to elevate your brand, expand your influence, and unlock new revenue streams, now is the time to take action. The most successful personal brands don't happen by accident—they are strategically built, positioned, and monetized. Whether you're an entrepreneur, speaker, coach, or business owner, I'll help you craft a powerful, celebrity-level brand that commands attention and drives results.

What You'll Gain Working With Me:

- A clear personal brand strategy that sets you apart in your industry.

- Monetization insights to turn your expertise into multiple income streams.

- Visibility and authority-building tactics that attract premium clients, media opportunities, and brand partnerships.

Let's Make It Happen:

- Book a consultation today and start executing your celebrity-level brand strategy → https://api.leadconnectorhq.com/widget/bookings/dradiscoverycall

- Visit For More Info: www.celebritybrandingusa.com

Your brand deserves the spotlight. This is your moment—take it.

About The Author

Dr. Catrise Austin, widely known as "The Queen of Smiles," is an award-winning celebrity cosmetic dentist, best-selling author, international speaker, brand spokesperson, and host of the Let's Talk Smiles Podcast and the Celebrity Branding Podcast. With years of expertise in dentistry and branding, she has been featured in Entrepreneur Magazine as well as on national platforms such as The Dr. Oz Show and The Today Show, sharing her expert insights on oral health and confidence.

In addition to transforming smiles, Dr. Austin is the founder of Celebrity Branding, an agency designed to help entrepreneurs stand out in their industries. Using her signature Fame Formula™, she guides clients to brand like a star, build influence like a leader, and monetize like a boss by helping them gain brand clarity, maximize their social media, launch books, create podcasts, secure media visibility, and attract ideal new clients. Her mission is to empower entrepreneurs to elevate their brands, gain nationwide recognition, and position their brands for a high value exit.

Whether she's crafting picture-perfect smiles or building celebrity brands, Dr. Austin's passion lies in helping others shine in their personal and professional lives.

Made in the USA
Monee, IL
17 April 2025

15444807R00079